How to Deal with a Narcissist

Learn to overcome manipulation and abuse

By

Ben Carlos

© **Copyright 2021 - All rights reserved.**

The content contained within this book may not be reproduced, duplicated or transmitted without direct written permission from the author or the publisher.

Under no circumstances will any blame or legal responsibility be held against the publisher, or author, for any damages, reparation, or monetary loss due to the information contained within this book, either directly or indirectly.

Legal Notice:

This book is copyright protected. It is only for personal use. You cannot amend, distribute, sell, use, quote or paraphrase any part, or the content within this book, without the consent of the author or publisher.

Disclaimer Notice:

Please note the information contained within this document is for educational and entertainment purposes only. All effort has been executed to present accurate, up to date, reliable, complete information. No warranties of any kind are declared or implied. Readers acknowledge that the author is not engaged in the rendering of legal, financial, medical or professional advice. The content within this book has been derived from various sources. Please consult a licensed professional before attempting any techniques outlined in this book.

By reading this document, the reader agrees that under no circumstances is the author responsible for any losses, direct or indirect, that are incurred as a result of the use of the information contained within this document, including, but not limited to, errors, omissions, or inaccuracies.

Table of Contents

Introduction	7
Chapter 1: Narcissistic Abuse	11
Chapter 2: Personality Traits of the Abuser	16
Chapter 3: Types of Abuse	23
Chapter 4: Types of Narcissistic Relationships	36
Chapter 5: Why Narcissists Victimize	43
Chapter 6: Breaking Free: Preparation	48
Chapter 7: Breaking Free: Leaving	53
Chapter 8: Breaking Free: Aftermath	59
Conclusion	66
References	71

Introduction

They are mothers, fathers, sons, or daughters. They are cousins, aunts, uncles, or friends. They are husbands, wives, lovers, or foes. They can be found working in any profession. Narcissists live and work among us, often going to great lengths in order to cover up who they truly are. What exactly is a narcissist? The term gets thrown around a lot regarding those with harsh personalities that have a tendency towards selfishness, but anyone who has dealt with narcissistic abuse knows a true narcissist goes far beyond that. Empathy is a completely foreign concept to these abusers; they are utterly unable to see a situation from a different perspective. They feel entitled to the attention, loyalty, money, and time of those who are unfortunate enough to get too close to them. Exploitation is second nature; it's common for a narcissist to let others do the work while they take credit.

The understanding of narcissism and narcissistic abuse is relatively new. Although there has been a lot of awareness regarding this type of person as of late, it is still very difficult to recognize them for who they are until it is often too late. The abuse is so gradual that it is hard for the victim to determine what is happening. These egomaniacs know who they are; they will do anything to cover up their traits and put on a good act upon first meeting. It typically takes about seven meetings until their true character shows.

It is estimated that they make up five percent of the population; that means they number over 12 million in the United States alone. If each of these individuals abuses five people in their lifetime, that makes a little over 60 million victims in the United States. That number is a conservative estimate; many narcissists have large families, employees, or subordinates working under them, or a large network of friends or acquaintances that all have the potential to be victimized at some point in their life.

Emotional scars linger years after narcissistic abuse has ended. Such relationships are very confusing, as the abuser can be so very loving and charming at times. Residual effects go much further than depression and anxiety; the victim is left to unravel the complex and inexplicable behavior of the narcissist as they attempt to answer the question, "why?" They often think there is something about their personality or behavior that invited the attention of such a cold-hearted person. Questions of their discernment abound as they wonder if there were red flags that should have been detected.

There is nothing wrong with the victim of narcissistic abuse; a narcissist is a master manipulator who can put on a convincing performance which differs depending on the type of person they wish to draw into their life.

Depression, anxiety, and confusion are only the tip of the iceberg. The victim is also swayed into giving up many aspects of their personal life such as their career, their friends, and their family. Narcissists thrive on creating a situation that makes their victim dependent in some way. Often, careers are given up because the narcissist needs someone to care for them, and a full-time job does not leave enough time. It's easier to lock a person into an abusive relationship when they have no money of their own and would have a difficult time finding work after a lengthy employment gap. They will find excuses as to why the victim cannot see or speak with friends or family until the relationships eventually wither. An outsider with no love for the narcissist is likely to see the situation for what it is and make continued attempts to steer their loved one in a different direction.

Severe mental abuse stunts the self-esteem of the victim long after the partnership is over. It's hard enough to summon the strength required to leave the relationship, but what comes after is just as difficult. There will be voices in the victim's head telling them they aren't good enough, don't know how to perform certain tasks, need constant help, and won't make it on their own. Although these voices are nothing but echoes from memories of an inadequate individual, it takes quite a bit of effort and insight to separate truth from lies. Only time, perseverance, and success achieving their goals will quiet those voices.

Chapter 1: Narcissistic Abuse

What is Narcissistic Abuse?

Subtlety is the name of the game; narcissists are masters at using underhanded tactics to abuse their victims. They seem to fly under the radar, free to wreak havoc upon a never ending string of unsuspecting victims. It's difficult to pinpoint exactly what the abuse is and even more difficult to bring the abuse to the attention of others. Rarely will the narcissist use physical violence as a means to terrorize; such a show of force will leave no doubt in the minds of those around them of what kind of person they truly are.

It's an uphill battle for the victim to get help or bring others over to their side during the abuse cycle. One of the hallmarks of this type of persecution is they are made to believe they cannot do anything right and always perceive things in the wrong way. It's not uncommon for victims to see themselves in the role of the villain, or at least as an inept individual who should thank their lucky stars that they have been taken under the wing of the narcissist. Narcissistic personality types don't often have many close friends. Because of this, it's not unheard of for only current and former victims to know the truth of how the narcissist behaves. They put on quite a convincing facade for acquaintances and co-workers, knowing that they would never make it far in life if those they rely on understood their true nature. Many times, attempts by the victim to seek outside help or advice are met with disbelief. The narcissist is very good at making excuses and playing to the crowd; it's likely that they would be able to convince others that the victim is actually the abuser.

Narcissistic abuse is very purposeful. Generally they hone in on one main victim at a time; if too many people are subjected to their methods at once, the collective cries for help might not go unnoticed. There is a cyclical pattern of abuse which repeats for each new victim.

Narcissistic Abuse Cycle

Relationships with a narcissist are so confusing, because the partnership and ways of interacting do not seem so vile at the onset. On the contrary, the victim often feels they have finally found the one who understands them. At first, there is an experience of a whirlwind of love; finally, someone has arrived who loves them so deeply and appears to understand them from the start. Narcissists know what they want and how they must conduct themselves to gain a specific partner. There are three main stages in the narcissistic abuse cycle: idealization, devaluation, and rejection.

Idealization

Any romantic relationship is rather different in the beginning than it is when the relationship matures. Both parties put their best foot forward, there is no emotional baggage, and no shared or mundane chores to attend. The honeymoon phase is a normal part of any relationship, but narcissists take this to an extreme. They make their eventual victim feel as if they are the face of perfection and can do no wrong. Perhaps this is true to an extent, as narcissists often look for those with positive qualities they feel are lacking in themselves. However, those positive attributes are not simply enjoyed within this type of relationship; the narcissist literally consumes their partner's beneficial qualities. One with a nurturing disposition will be pushed to take care of the narcissist, while another with a plethora of monetary resources will need to continually spend in order to keep the affection of the charlatan. An educated teacher can do nothing but instruct the narcissist, while the fun-loving spirit is forced to be continual entertainment. It's often the case that the victim begins to despise those positive qualities in themselves that have seemingly become their downfall.

Devaluation

In this stage the narcissist has already gleaned what they could from the relationship. The focus changes to what the victim doesn't have; suddenly, the narcissist sees them as the imperfect human that we all are. Settling into a mundane routine and accepting the limits of their partner is not something that can be expected from a narcissist. They demand perfection, but that is not possible in a long-term relationship. Nobody is perfect in every aspect; everyone needs a pause to rest and unwind. When the caretaker needs a break, the tycoon wants to focus their resources in another direction. The teacher wishes to learn, or when the party-planner wants their own entertainment is when the mask begins to slip, and more obvious types of abuse come into play. During this stage, the narcissist will point out any and all flaws, both real and perceived.

The victim feels they can do nothing right and is left scratching their head, trying to figure out who this person is that used to think so highly of them.

Rejection

Narcissists will take what they can and inflict harm when there is nothing else to acquire from the relationship. The third and final stage of rejection typically doesn't occur until a new mark with new positive attributes to be consumed enters the scene. The victim is left feeling confused, humiliated, and often with a sense of self-loathing for what makes them special. On occasion, a victim figures out the game before rejection can occur and ends the relationship or calls out the narcissist. In these instances, what follows is narcissistic rage. When their facade is shown to be nothing but a sham, they are forced to see themselves as inadequate and vulnerable; their delusion of grandeur is crushed when this non-perfect person doesn't want anything to do with them. A victim must take great care if they are the one to end the relationship. Narcissists are very vindictive and will often slander their former partner in a last ditch attempt to save face.

Chapter 2: Personality Traits of the Abuser

Personality of the Abuser

To an outsider, the narcissist may seem to have it all: confidence, a large circle of friends, an important job, and a devoted family. Upon taking a closer look, however, all of these positive attributes are nothing but a pretense. Having mastered the art of storytelling and lies, the narcissist puts considerable effort into how they are perceived. Underneath a shiny veneer of perfection, they are nothing but a scared individual with low self-esteem attempting to distract others from seeing their true self. More than that, the narcissist hides from themself, refusing to see and acknowledge any negative qualities. For this reason, an unsuspecting victim is always needed; there must be someone on whom to place the blame for unsavory aspects of their own personality.

True narcissism is recognized as a personality disorder. Above all, these individuals completely lack empathy. They are not able to put themselves into another's shoes; looking at a situation from another point of view is an impossibility. Forever entitled, they frequently use others to obtain what they desire. When a victim has nothing else to offer, they are lucky to merely be discarded; often the narcissist will use slander and attack their reputation so that nobody will believe them if they attempt to speak the truth. Conversations with the narcissist tend to be one-sided; it can be hard to get a word in edgewise. It can seem that the only time they truly listen is when information can be gleaned that will be used against the victim at a later time. Those around the narcissist are expected to do their bidding; if this doesn't happen, they can become enraged. "No," is never an acceptable response; complete obedience is necessary to any ongoing relationship.

Narcissists think very highly of themselves; their sense of influence and authority are massively bloated. Everything is theirs for the taking; in their mind, they are the most worthy, so why would anyone expect something other than the crumbs to be left behind? Because they believe themselves to be special, they will only associate with other highly influential people. Everything has to be the best; cars, clothes, hobbies, and careers cannot be seen as subpar. Those they see as beneath them are viewed as inferior and only exist to be used.

Such high standards in every aspect of life are not able to be achieved, at least not long-term. Real friendships and familial relationships aren't possible when those involved with the narcissist can never measure up. Of course, the narcissist is hateful towards their close circle, but there is also at least a bit of resentment that those around feel towards the narcissist, even if they haven't completely figured out the game. The failure of the narcissist to control emotions and behavior eventually drives most people away. Although they can put on quite a show of importance, they are quite often lonely. Change is torturous, and stress is not something they manage appropriately. Usually, there is a tendency towards depression, as they can never measure up to their own high standards. Shame, humiliation, and insecurity are what hide beneath their mask of perfection. Of course, feeling those sentiments of inadequacy too deeply isn't something a narcissist will allow to happen, so they project their own shortcomings onto their chosen victims.

Types of Narcissists

Overt

This is the easiest type to spot; they can be seen from a mile away. They are loud. They are boastful. They are show-offs. Everything about their demeanor is a huge red flag, but they know how to have fun and be the life of the party, allowing them to rope in their victims. Any attention is good attention; being perceived negatively is not such a problem as long as they are noticed and remembered. This type generally knows who they are and the pain they inflict upon others. They may not describe themselves as a narcissist, but they understand their tendency to use and abuse whoever they can. This type is most prone to narcissistic rage; physical abuse, as well as emotional abuse, is common.

Covert

This type is a bit harder to spot unless they are known personally. While the overt narcissist displays extroverted tendencies, the covert narcissist tends to be quite introverted. Forever the victim, they always have someone to blame for life's unfair circumstances. It's common for covert narcissists to have a history of depression and anxiety. Illness and negative events are overly embellished to gain attention and sympathy; they are masterful actors who can often cry on cue. It's quite difficult to catch this type in a lie; they cover their tracks well and are very careful with their actions. They typically set their sights on those with a caretaker personality, often draining them financially as well as emotionally.

Communal

Flying under the radar, utilizing a guise of helpfulness and community-mindedness, the communal narcissist could be a politician, PTA mother, or the leader of a non-profit organization. Holding delusions of grandeur not only about themselves personally but about what they have to offer to their community or the world at large is what defines a communal narcissist. Everyone acts in their own self-interest to some extent, so what sets them apart from others in highly visible community roles, and why are they a detriment to the communities they claim to serve? The primary defining characteristic of a narcissist is a lack of empathy. They don't actually understand those around them and often look down on individuals they perceive as beneath them. Because of this, communal narcissists will never achieve their supposed goal of benefiting their community or those suffering hardships. It's impossible to help someone without understanding their plight and without looking at them as another human being, deserving of respect and dignity. Their cause is important in giving them a reason for their feelings of superiority; those who work with them are surprised when the mask slips and it becomes painfully obvious they care more for attention and personal gain than the community or organizational goals. It's often the case that those closest to them bear the brunt of their narcissistic traits. Public figures must be very careful with the image they show the world. Communal narcissists often take their anger out on their families behind closed doors. Families of these types have a very tough time; it's often hard for outsiders to believe that such an upstanding and giving role model could be abusive in their private life.

Antagonistic

Everything is a competition with this type of narcissist; their laser-sharp focus rests almost entirely on rivalry. They share many traits with overt narcissists but tend to see their victims not as lesser individuals to be used, but as competitors to be defeated. Romantic relationships are not as common and are short-lived. They can be quite paranoid, thinking everyone is out to get them. Although all narcissists have at least some antagonistic tendencies, this type is always out to prove themselves, and they keep score over anything and everything.

Malignant

Perhaps the most destructive type, the malignant narcissist is downright sadistic; it's incredibly hard to differentiate between malignant narcissists and psychopaths. They are very stubborn with fairly simplistic views; everything is black or white, good or bad, friend or foe. Reveling in the pain inflicted upon others, they will never apologize unless it can be seen as advantageous in some way. This type is the most likely to physically abuse their victims.

Chapter 3: Types of Abuse

Gaslighting

Perhaps the most common type of abuse employed by the narcissist, gaslighting is emotional manipulation that makes the abused think they are not perceiving things correctly. At times, the victim may even believe they are losing their sanity. Their own memories become unreliable, as the narcissist is able to undermine personal experience and implant false information and different means of interpretation. This causes the victim to imagine they are inept and unable to function in the world without help from their abuser. They can remain stuck in an imaginary prison created by the narcissist for an absurd amount of time when all the while they are competent enough to set themselves free.

In the 1930s and 1940s, a theatrical performance and movie called *Gaslight* coined the term, which has gained traction and understanding in modern times. In this production, written by Patrick Hamilton, a husband dims the gaslights in their home each evening. When his wife asks him why he did it, he is adamant that he did no such thing and the lights look the same as always. In addition, he embeds fictitious events into her memory, spinning a tale that her mother was mentally unstable, heard voices, and eventually died in a mental institution. Eventually, the wife thinks she is losing her mind and is not perceiving things around her correctly. She must walk on eggshells, as her husband's hot temper comes and goes randomly. This work was truly ahead of its time; little did Patrick Hamilton know that nearly 100 years later, there would be revival performances all over the world as people finally understood narcissistic abuse and the pain it inflicts.

Gaslighting happens little by little, and in small doses at first. Seeds of self-doubt are planted; this causes the abuse to be easily concealed and often go undetected. The narcissist will gaslight a victim over very mundane things, which often go unquestioned, because it's difficult to understand why one would lie about inconsequential details that have no bearing on life. There are several different types of gaslighting: countering, withholding, trivializing, denial, diverting, and stereotyping.

Countering

This technique seeks to undermine thoughts and memories. "I don't remember it like that," or, "Your memory has always been off," are common phrases that make the victim question themselves. Countering typically begins over benign subjects that don't have much effect on either party; its only purpose is to cause the victim to be less sure of themselves in all situations. The narcissist will often declare opinions that clash with those on the receiving end of their abuse, no matter what they truly believe. Narcissists wish for the victim to always feel as if they are wrong and eventually unable to believe their own perceptions.

Withholding

The ultimate control mechanism, withholding, happens when the narcissist identifies something their victim needs or desires and keeps it just out of reach. This is one of the methods used when inflicting financial abuse, although money is not the only thing that can be used with this tactic. Information can be withheld, making the victim feel silly for not knowing something after the abuser asserts that the information was given. At times, this tactic can go as far as the silent treatment; the narcissist may refuse to look at or even recognize the presence of their victim. The silent treatment is particularly cruel because there is no way to know exactly why the narcissist is angry. Often, the victim will end up apologizing without understanding the perceived slight just to make the abuse stop. Being ignored is psychological torture for one that has been isolated from all others in their life.

Trivializing

"You're too sensitive." "It's really not a big deal." These phrases are commonplace in narcissistic relationships; acting just like rubber, the narcissist will throw any fault or blame back onto their victim in an attempt to resist accountability. They may admit to a portion of the wrongdoing—never the most serious issue—so that it seems they are taking some sort of responsibility. The emotions of the victim are belittled and blamed on a distorted fault within them. Trivializing, also referred to as minimization, does two things; it takes the attention away from what the victim understands as a problem, and it belittles or finds fault instead with the victim. When one uses this tactic, it is a sure thing they will repeat the offense in question.

An example of trivializing would be when a narcissist physically shoves their partner. They may admit to a slight push but will deny that the touch went so far as to cause any type of harm. They will then bring up what the victim did prior to being shoved and say they were asking for it.

Denial/Diversion

This tactic is similar to trivialization, except that the narcissist denies even a small part of wrongdoing, and instead changes the topic to a fault found with the victim. The narcissist never takes accountability for their actions; if they are called out for an action or comment that is unacceptable, they often will not admit to it at all. It's impossible to have any sort of valid discussion when one party refuses to discuss any qualms their partner may have about them by deploying the tactic of denial.

Typically coming on the heels of denial, diversion is used to change the subject. Because their victims have had seeds of self-doubt planted through gaslighting over benign issues, they may eventually believe that they did not observe the situation correctly. Any attempt to discuss a narcissist's negative and harmful actions will always result in a discussion of their victim's real or imagined problematic behavior.

Stereotyping

A person's race, gender, or sexuality is used against them to discourage them from seeking help. A female victim will be told that she sounds irrational, and nobody will believe her. A male victim will be told that he needs to toughen up, or that real men can't be abused. It makes the victim believe that the whole world holds the same views as the narcissist.

Compliments and Gifts

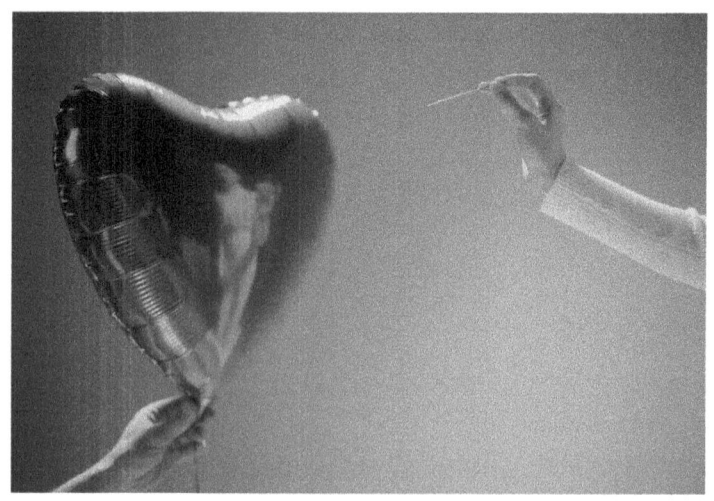

This is a common tactic used in virtually all types of narcissistic relationships in order to completely draw their victim in so they won't attempt to go elsewhere to seek affection. Usually occurring in the idealization stage, unless being utilized to keep the victim off-center later in the relationship. The narcissist may give expensive jewelry for no apparent reason early in the relationship or send multiple flower arrangements to the workplace. Constant compliments expounding on the victim's perfection, or expressing love at an inappropriately early time in the relationship, are more red flags. The narcissist will call or text continually, even when they know the victim is busy and unable to respond. Most new couples communicate often, but needing to be in constant contact nearly every hour of the day is done out of a need for control. The narcissist's need to be the sole target of one's attention is an isolation tactic that is not as sweet as it may first seem.

Isolation

In the early days of any relationship, most people choose to self-isolate to some extent with their new partner. This is to be expected as the two get to know one another and settle into a routine. However, narcissists will often sabotage the established personal and professional relationships of their partner, so they will have nowhere to turn when the relationship takes a turn for the worse. It is easier to keep control when the victim is dependent upon them for money, a social life, or information. Once the abuse is obvious, the victim often keeps themselves in isolation out of shame. It can be embarrassing that they allowed older relationships to falter for someone who quickly turned abusive. It's also possible that friends or family saw the narcissist for who they are and tried to give warning. The victim may feel ashamed that they didn't take the advice and leave before any real damage was done.

Verbal Abuse

When verbal abuse is spewed from a narcissist, it is absolutely crushing for those on the receiving end. It's a choice tactic of master manipulators that serves many purposes. Primarily, verbal abuse is utilized to intimidate, claim dominance, and instill fear. The reasoning for such action is all over the place; typically, many perceived faults are addressed in quick succession, preventing the victim from forming any sort of coherent response. Often, some truth is infused with the overblown faults addressed in the tirade, which increases the confusion and inability to properly respond. The pitch and volume of their voice can vary from ear-splitting to whisper silent depending on the situation at hand. Also included with this type of abuse are more benign tactics, such as withholding information, interrupting, and interrogation.

Financial Abuse

Financial abuse is so widespread among narcissists, and is so prevalent among all types of relationships that it must be broken up into several categories.

Asset Narcissists

This type will lavish their victim with gifts and access to money only to demand complete submission. Guilt-tripping is heavily deployed in these instances; they say since so much money has been spent on the victim, the least that can be done is to go along with whatever it is they want. They make it difficult to refuse gifts by preventing the victim from working or accessing their own resources. As retribution for disobedience, they will refuse to pay their partners financial obligations such as child support, health insurance, or car insurance; the victim is then left vulnerable to legal penalties.

Banking/Credit Narcissists

This type has no qualms with committing fraud; they are known to steal the victim's paycheck and place it in an inaccessible bank account, leaving the victim completely dependent. Some will open and max out credit cards in their partner's name, ensuring years of debt and financial obligations even after the relationship ends. The victim is not given accurate information—if they are given any information at all—regarding investment accounts and secret caches of money.

Budgeting Narcissists

Guilt regarding spending habits is used by this type to feel superior to their partner. They often give an allowance that is impossible to live on to justify their control over finances. A budgeting narcissist may shame their partner for the purchase of a much needed pair of shoes while they buy a new gaming system. A stay-at-home parent may be criticized for their spending habits even though they are responsible for all household purchases and bought nothing for themselves.

Work-Related Narcissists

Instead of outright refusing to allow their partners to work, this type often sabotages their job by showing up unannounced, calling excessively, or stealing the car keys so their partner is eventually fired. Sometimes, they will force their partners to work for them for very low pay while preventing them from going to school or seeking outside employment.

Chapter 4: Types of Narcissistic Relationships

Romantic

Doubtlessly, the most common type of narcissistic relationship, a romantic union with a narcissist, is full of turmoil. One of the most difficult concepts to accept is that the narcissist never truly loves their partner. One must love themselves in order to love another, and narcissists act the way they do because of a lack of self-love. It's heart-wrenching for the victim, because there are often many good times in the beginning of the relationship. Narcissists do tend to be a lot of fun at times, and often enjoy certain special connections.

Although some narcissists do marry, many fear commitment and are unable to remain satiated with one partner after the initial honeymoon phase. Generally, they have one or more future love interests in the back of their mind to attach themselves to when the relationship begins to dissolve. This is called a narcissistic supply; they are unable to cope without someone to emotionally feed from.

Parent/Child

Children of narcissistic parents have a tough time growing up, as their parents tend to live vicariously through them and use them as a measure of their own self-worth. It's not uncommon for the parent to have their child's whole life planned before they are even out of diapers, knowing exactly what will impress others. Obviously, this is quite hard on the child who is always aware that they will never quite measure up to their parent's grandiose vision. Anxiety is common in these children, since they are never given the freedom to make their own choices or truly be themselves.

These children are given far too much responsibility regarding the family status and must always exhibit perfection. Narcissists can't stand for their mask of superiority to slip, and children are not as apt at maintaining the perception of impeccability. Making mistakes as a teenager is gut-wrenching because of the disappointment of the parent and the shame that will bring.

Narcissistic parents can be cruel, and their children are generally unable to seek help, at least at a young age. First of all, being raised in that environment makes it seem normal. The child will likely be older before they realize their family life is anything but normal. Also, who would believe that the seemingly sweet woman who volunteers at their school and takes part in every fundraiser is abusive? Finally, even if the child were to be believed, nothing could be done in the absence of physical harm. All that would be accomplished from speaking out is more shame and verbal abuse.

A cruel demeanor is not always the case. Quite often, a narcissistic parent can be amiable and affectionate, but there are always conditions to be met. Narcissists can come close to truly loving their child, but conditional love is never absolute and true.

This type of relationship is particularly damaging due to the amount of control a parent has over their child. Even as the child grows into an adult, the parent often retains a large amount of power over them. This is due to several factors, one being a lifetime of gaslighting. The child has grown up to believe they are incapable and need this parent to make it in the world. There is often a fair amount of guilt-tripping when the child tries to make their own decisions; the parent often brings up how they cared for the child and gifts that were given with the expectation that their child must repay them as an adult with unending loyalty.

The Narcissistic Mother

When the mother is the narcissistic parent rather than the father, a whole crop of additional insecurities and hardships are sure to be experienced by the children. It's politically correct to say that both parents are equal in the amount of nurturing and care given to children, but that is not usually the case, especially in families in which both parents are involved. The mother should be the soft spot where a child can rest in safety and comfort.

As babies, they find safety snuggled on her chest, feeling her breath. As preschoolers, they find comfort in her arms, crying over a scraped knee after taking the training wheels off the bike. As an adolescent, they find comfort after a break-up by resting their head on her shoulder. As an adult, they find comfort talking to their mother over the phone when problems arise at work. That's how it should be, at least. Children of narcissistic mothers have no soft place to go to for comfort. They have no place where it's safe to let their guard down, nowhere to go when they make mistakes. Children of narcissistic mothers have learned over the years that it is not safe to open up and speak freely to her; she remembers every word of those conversations and will use it at the first opportunity to make her child feel guilty or inept. They have always understood that mistakes are not opportunities used for teaching; if their mother becomes aware of a mistake, it will only mean blame and shame are soon to follow.

Those who suffered under the care of a narcissistic mother tend to have a lot of relationship troubles later in life. They are extreme people-pleasers, always putting themselves last. They have grown up without knowing what true love and acceptance feels like; they are always trying, but never feel they are quite good enough. This puts them at risk of getting involved romantically with a narcissist and experiencing a whole new cycle of abuse.

Workplace

Narcissism in the workplace is a relatively new understanding; those with such attitudes were previously referred to as harsh bosses or difficult co-workers. It is becoming clear that such individuals are not only harmful to those they work with, but also to the community that the corporation serves.

Narcissistic leaders can negatively affect a corporation even years after they are gone. They poison the organizational culture in a number of ways. They blame, abuse, and create conflict. Employees are often harassed and abused, leaving them in a less than ideal mental state. There tends to be a significant pay gap, not only among them and their subordinates, but also between them and other non-narcissistic leaders. This is due largely to their habit of taking credit for the work and ideas of others. Companies that employ narcissistic leaders become entangled in more lawsuits than other institutions. There is little collaboration among the workforce with a narcissist at the lead. Those who wish to work together are targeted by the narcissist and often leave the organization, taking their talents elsewhere.

Chapter 5: Why Narcissists Victimize

Whole Object Relations

Narcissists have a vision in mind of how their partner, child, friend, or employee should look and behave. The mental concept they hold is one of perfection that is impossible for anyone to achieve. They are unable to see the person—the whole object—as they exist in the real world, a mixture of positive and negative qualities. In their mind, everyone is either good or bad. This mindset is far removed from reality. Every person is a mixture of both strengths and weaknesses; that is what it means to be human. Once the narcissist gains awareness of a negative quality, they are unable to remember any positive attributes and are willing to throw the whole person away. Unfortunately, they often become so enraged at the imperfection, and what that mirrors back to them about their own inadequacies, that they seek to destroy their victims in whatever way possible before discarding them.

Object Consistency

Relationships, just like the people involved, are a medley of positives and negatives. The act of involvement in a relationship means that there are good times, laughs, and love. Arguments, setbacks, and disagreements also tend to be part of the mix. Narcissists are unable to remember the good times when they experience a setback. Because their mind works in this way, they believe that their partner also has a similar thought process. The fear of abandonment is intense for a narcissist; this leads them to lash out and walk away before the same happens to them.

Personality Disorder

Narcissistic Personality Disorder (NPD) is a recognized mental disorder. Officially, it is classified as a rare disease, with fewer than 200,000 cases in the United States per year. There seems to be a disconnect between diagnosed cases and the number of supposed narcissists most people come across in their lives. This could be explained in two ways. First of all, a defining factor in determining whether or not somebody has NPD is an inflated sense of superiority; a person who sees themselves as perfect will be unlikely to speak to a therapist, much less accept a diagnosis for a mental illness. If they do seek help, it is often for related problems such as depression or drug/alcohol abuse.

Also, it's important to understand that just about everybody exhibits narcissistic traits to some degree at some point in their lives. Confidence, high standards, and high self-esteem are an important part of being a well-adjusted adult. Most people are guilty of belittling others or becoming envious at some point in time. What sets true narcissists apart from average people having a bad moment or getting through a rough patch in life is the time frame that negative narcissistic traits are exhibited and the long-term damage done to relationships. Whole object relations and object permanence are important defining factors as to whether or not someone is a bona fide narcissist. The root cause of narcissism remains unknown; there are theories that it is caused by genetics, the environment, or childhood trauma, but the jury is still out. We do know that males are more likely to suffer from NPD than females, and that the disorder presents itself in the teenage or early adult years.

Lack of Relationship Modeling

Many narcissists have troubled childhoods in some way or another. Some come from abusive homes where one parent harmed the other, either emotionally or physically. Others were forced to grow up too fast by taking care of younger siblings during what should have been their childhood, and yet others may have been coddled too much and were given everything without doing anything to deserve it. Maybe, instead of being consoled when they cried, their parents locked them in a room alone until they calmed down. This does not make their harmful actions as an adult acceptable, but it may provide an insight to their victims and bring some sort of solace that they are not the reason for the abuse. It's important to note that not everyone is in a position to make a clean break from a narcissist, never having to deal with them again. Unfortunately, narcissists exist in all places, and sometimes, it's necessary to learn how to handle them over time. Understanding what made them the way they are is a good method to cope with such a task.

Chapter 6: Breaking Free: Preparation

Once a decision is made to leave a narcissist, it's important to make preparations in advance so that the actual act of leaving is done as quickly as possible. This should be done quietly, so as to not bring the plan to their awareness. They are likely to do anything they can to force their partner to stay, making it nearly impossible to leave with hope of rebuilding a life. There is also the chance they could become physically violent. Before making any preparations, it's essential that the victim ensures there are no tracking devices or spy software programs installed on their cell phone or vehicle. If there is no way for such devices to be removed without alerting the abuser, a burner phone will be needed, along with funds for ride-shares during this phase. Create a new email address and begin having all electronic correspondence transferred.

Living Arrangements

It's likely that the narcissist has isolated their victim, and the few friendships and family relations remaining are strained. That doesn't mean there is nowhere to turn; consider those who showed concern and were vocal about their dislike of the abuser. It's reasonable to assume they are willing to help, but have to wait on the sidelines until the victim makes the decision to leave. There has to be somewhere to go, a friend with a sleeper sofa or a parent with an extra bedroom. If there is nobody willing or able to help, they should look into extended stay hotels or call a domestic violence hotline for assistance. Even if the victim has funds and the ability to secure housing from the start, it will be difficult to do so while living under the same roof as the narcissist without letting their plan become known. Move possessions little by little at carefully planned times. Nothing that the narcissist will notice missing should be moved until the victim is ready to leave for good.

Financial Arrangements

Even if there is a solid plan for housing, money will be needed; many narcissists do not allow their partners to work for this reason. The victim will have an easier time if they open a secret bank account, ensuring that no paper statements are sent through the mail. There is currently a plethora of entry-level work from home jobs that can at least provide money for food and transportation while a friend helps out with housing. Perhaps a neighbor needs a babysitter, or someone to provide lawn care; anything that could quietly bring in some income should be taken into consideration. Keep an eye out for small amounts of cash in the house that won't be missed. Many victims will have a problem with this, as they are usually good-hearted people who would never steal, but if the narcissist has not allowed them to work, a bit of money here and there doesn't even begin to pay for lost wages.

Support System

It's vital to have some sort of support system in place after breaking free from a narcissist. It will likely take some time to become strong enough to live independently, and having friends or family close by will lessen the desire to return to a comfortable prison. It's helpful to network through friends in order to find meaningful and well-paying work; getting back into a career after a long absence is difficult. There are also free hotlines where the victim could find a sympathetic ear or help locate resources and career opportunities.

Special Considerations

If children are involved, the victim cannot just disappear without a trace. They can, however, prepare themselves for a custody battle before the narcissist knows of their plan to leave. Children deserve both parents in their life, but when dealing with a narcissist, the rules are a bit different. If any abuse has been aimed at a child, their welfare depends on being protected by the fleeing parent. Even if there is no history of abuse towards the child, the situation needs to be closely monitored. A narcissist requires a victim; if the partner is no longer around, it is entirely possible that a child could end up on the receiving end. It's important to keep detailed records of every bit of emotional or physical abuse. Save text messages, emails, and voicemail. Perhaps it would be helpful to keep a journal, detailing the abuse as it occurs, including names of those who witnessed the mistreatment. If the narcissist is involved in any illegal activity, proof should be gathered, as long as it is safe to do so.

In cases of narcissistic parents, it may not be possible or desirable to cut ties entirely. It's important to establish strict boundaries and ensure they are enforced. The harsh reality is that it's extremely unlikely that the parent will ever change or apologize. Accept it and let go. It's more important that the victim get on with their own life instead of trying to work miracles. They should fully understand and recognize abuse tactics, such as gaslighting, and resist any attempts the parent makes at gaining control. Children of narcissistic parents will need to learn to parent themselves. Although unfair, it is a vital part of healing.

Chapter 7: Breaking Free: Leaving

Choosing the Right Time

The right time to leave is whenever the abuser will be unaware of the whereabouts of the victim for the longest period of time. Perhaps it will be at the start of their longest workday, or directly after leaving on a weekend fishing trip with friends. Gather important information such as birth certificates, passports, and titles to property in the victim's name.

Blocking

Personal access should never be willingly granted to the narcissist after leaving. The narcissist likely still has ways to check up on their victim, but it should be made as difficult as possible in hopes they lose interest. They should be blocked from all social media and from calling, even if the victim acquired a new phone number.

Change All Passwords

Great care should be taken to change all passwords to something the narcissist would be unable to guess. Even if the victim does not believe that their abuser knows certain passwords, it is always surprising what these individuals find out during a relationship. Social media, banks, and email are a given, but they shouldn't forget to change passwords for online shopping and grocery pickup as well. A new address will not stay secret for long if the abuser can determine where new work clothes are being shipped.

Log Out of All Devices

Typically changing passwords will automatically log out of all devices, but it's always best to take extra precautions to ensure safety. It may be difficult to use the cell phone of the abuser, but an attempt should be made to do so. Perhaps it's possible for the victim to "lose" their phone and ask to check their email or social media. Have a list of sites that could provide a forwarding address and quickly log off each one.

Block "Flying Monkeys"

A flying monkey is a term to describe the people a narcissist uses to gather information, perform damage control, distribute misinformation, or anything else that helps ensnare and harm the narcissist's victims. The term comes from *The Wizard of Oz;* the Wicked Witch of the West kept flying monkeys under her spell in order to harm Dorothy. It's vital that flying monkeys are unable to reach or check up on the victim after the escape. Just like the narcissist, they should be blocked on social media and from calling. The victim needs to make sure anyone who is part of their support system is aware of these individuals, as the narcissist may send them to check with their friends and family in an attempt to hone in on a location.

Check For Tracking Devices

This should have been done during the preparation phase, but it should be done again upon leaving. Narcissists are master manipulators; even if they don't let on that they are aware of any preparations to leave, it is entirely possible that they caught onto something out of the ordinary. If that is the case, there is always a possibility that a tracking device has been recently planted on the victim's cell phone or vehicle. Tracking devices have to be installed on the smartphone that is to be tracked. Every app that is not used should be deleted, as well as any app the victim does not remember installing. Each remaining app needs to be opened to ensure it is what the victim believes it to be.

If the victim owns a vehicle that will be used in the escape, they will need to check for physical tracking devices. An electronic sweeper can be utilized for this task, and the victim may find such a gadget provides comfort by allowing them to frequently and easily check their vehicle and living quarters after leaving. In the absence of a sweeper, they can use a flashlight and check the entire undercarriage and wheel wells. A mirror with a long handle will be helpful for this. Any plastic covers should be removed to check the area underneath; battery operated tracking devices are magnetic and will need to be attached to metal if placed on the outside of the vehicle. It's unlikely that a device would be concealed under the hood due to high temperatures, but the victim should check anyway for peace of mind. Some trackers can be hidden in the interior of the car; common areas of concealment are under the dashboard, in the trunk near the spare tire, or under the seats. Most snoops utilizing a tracking device want to be able to install and remove as quickly as possible, so they are most likely to be installed on the outside of the vehicle near the edges. It can be helpful to ask a professional, as many people don't know exactly what they are looking for. Any auto industry professional who deals with electronics can assist in the search. Those who install remote starts, security, or audio systems can be helpful.

Get Rid of Gifts/Reminders

This is a time of looking forward, not back. After all the abuse, the victim should be happy to get rid of anything that would bring back memories of this time. Expensive jewelry or clothes gifted to the victim can be sold to assist in financing their new start in life. Pawn shops, consignment stores, or online marketplaces are good places to relieve themself of unwanted mementos. Photos and letters from this relationship should not be allowed into the future. Digital messages and photos need to be deleted, and their physical counterparts would make nice fuel for a fire in a personal rebirth ceremony.

Chapter 8: Breaking Free: The Aftermath

Self-Care and Self-Sufficiency

A survivor of narcissistic abuse needs to realize that what they have been through and the strength it took to break free is a big deal. It's no small task to build a new life from the ground up, and therefore, it's essential to take some time for self-care. What that entails is entirely up to the individual, and it may take some time to figure out exactly what that looks like. The victim has just come out of a relationship that was all about their partner. They should try different activities to see what feels right for them. Maybe they would like to take up a hobby or sport; they should sign up for a class or team to try it out. Sometimes self-care is as simple as a nightly walk and a bubble bath with a fizzy bath bomb. It's vital to have time that is only for the mental wellness of the victim; it is a way of retraining their mind that they matter and have great importance.

Self-sufficiency is connected to self-care; when they are able to provide for themselves, it's a massive boost to their self-esteem. There is a lot to learn, so it's important for the victim to realize that some mistakes will likely be made along the way. Also, it will probably take some time to attain the level of monetary comfort that they used to have. Networking with associates and acquaintances of friends and family will help to find a starter job. Victims should keep in mind that they are under no obligation to stay at any job for a long period of time; as long as nobody is hurt and no rules are broken, they are free to do what they like with their new life. They should try to get a job quickly that will help pay the bills and put some current working experience on their resume, but they should never stop looking for an opportunity to step into a new position with better benefits. They should also learn to maintain their vehicle, cook, or learn to be a bit more handy around the house. They were imprisoned by the narcissist; sometimes, imprisonment involves keeping one ignorant of various life-skills. They should never feel bad about themselves for not knowing how to do certain things; because of their strength in getting out of an abusive relationship, they will have no problem learning.

No Response

If all goes according to plan, the narcissist and their flying monkeys will be unable to locate the victim. That's not always the case due to certain circumstances, such as small town living where everybody knows everybody, or situations where children are involved. A visit or a phone call from the narcissist should never elicit any response other than "go away." If they continue to harass, the victim can go to the police and request an order of protection. This is why it's so important to keep good notes of any abuse, stalking, or harassment. A narcissist thrives off of attention and strife; they love to make their victims uncomfortable. The best response is no response; don't give them what they are after, and they will be more likely to lose interest.

Talk About It

It's usually helpful to talk about the ordeal at some point, although when and how that happens is completely up to the victim. Some may wish to discuss their former situation with trusted friends, family, or a therapist right away. This can be helpful to those supporting the victim in the first months of freedom by ensuring they understand the level of abuse this person endured. However, some need time to personally process what they went through, and they should never be rushed or pressured into talking until they are ready. It's imperative that the victim be given agency over every aspect of their life; when and how to discuss prior abuse needs to happen on the timeline of the victim's choosing.

Don't Rush

A victim should never compare themselves to anyone else or feel the need to achieve certain goals by an arbitrary date. Abuse inflicted by a narcissist is unlike any other type of abuse. Their whole way of thinking and living will need to be completely changed, and this does not happen overnight. They should never judge themselves by their living situation, what kind of car they drive, their job, or how big—or small—their circle of friends happens to be. The successful business person with a fancy house and car can be someone to admire if that's what the victim eventually wants in life, but it's important to remember that it's unlikely that role model endured the same level of abuse for so long. The victim must learn to give themselves some grace, which may seem a foreign concept after such treatment.

Relationships should not be rushed into either. It's crucial that the victim learns what they truly want in a partner; this is usually only achieved after a good amount of time for introspection. Much time and energy has been spent coddling another who was so very undeserving. The victim needs some time where all of their efforts are expended solely on themselves. Self-sufficiency is an integral part of their new life, and will make it less likely that they will be used and abused in such a way again. Anyone worth having in life is going to be willing to wait until they are ready.

Better Days Ahead

The first days, weeks, and months after leaving a narcissistic relationship will be exhilarating; there are so many new experiences, and the feeling of freedom is out of this world. However, after some time, the difficulties of starting over will become apparent. Life is expensive, especially now, and financial stress can be difficult for an adult just starting over in the world. One of the biggest mental blocks to get over is feeling the need to impress another. That way of thinking needs to go out the window; the focus is now on self-empowerment. It can also be quite lonely for one fresh out of an abusive relationship. After years of isolation, their social circle will be very small and possibly nonexistent. These problems will not last forever; money and friendships need time to flourish. Everyone feels down on themselves from time to time, but wallowing in self-pity will lead to nothing but trouble. When these feelings arise, the victim should remember the past and how much better off they are now. They should recall those first weeks of freedom when the world was theirs and the feeling of having the world at their fingertips was palpable. Better days are ahead; this is only the beginning.

Conclusion

There will be a calm after the storm. Leaving a relationship rife with both blatant and underhanded abuse is a complex problem; it's normal for emotional scars to remain years after the abuse. Although there is no easy solution, there is always a way out. One who can endure, recognize, and extricate themselves from such a dire situation has more strength than most people could ever comprehend. Victims of narcissistic abuse are true warriors and will eventually be able to rebuild their lives in a manner of their choosing.

It's vital that victims reflect on their encounter with narcissism. They can expect to feel pained as they relive the strained relationship, but it will serve them in the future. When the memories are reflected upon with a fresh outlook, they will gain an understanding of the actions of that disturbed character that will help them to recognize red flags of possible abusers in the future.

The world is a bright place with ample opportunities for growth and development. Many former victims of narcissistic abuse find themselves drawn to some sort of social work where their harsh experience can be used to help others who find themselves in similar circumstances. It's truly awe-inspiring how a person can endure such hardship and refuse to allow those experiences to harden their heart or instill cruelty in them. They tend to be kind, gentle, and understanding, an asset to anyone they wish to involve in their lives.

Help is Available

If you or someone you love has fallen victim to narcissistic abuse or domestic violence, please do not hesitate to reach out for help. There are various programs that exist to help victims achieve safety and independence. You can call 2-1-1 from anywhere in the United States for information about resources near you.

National Hotlines

National Domestic Abuse Hotline

1-800-799-SAFE

www.TheHotline.org

Supplemental Nutrition Assistance Program (SNAP)

1-800-221-5689

Volunteers of America (housing assistance)

www.voa.org

National Sexual Assault Hotline

1-800-656-4673

Childhelp National Child Abuse Hotline

800-422-4453

National Alliance on Mental Illness

1-800-950-NAMI

Crisis Text Hotline

Text CONNECT to 741741

Depression Hotline

1-630-482-9696

Stalking Hotlines

1-866-869-HELP

1-800-621-HOPE

References

Bonchay, B. (2017, June 2). Narcissistic Abuse Affects Over 158 Million People in the U.S. PsychCentral. https://psychcentral.com/lib/narcissistic-abuse-affects-over-158-million-people-iu-s#3n-the-

Butts, M. (2020, October 9). How Narcissistic Leaders Make Organizations Less Ethical. Greater Good Magazine; Berkeley University. https://greatergood.berkeley.edu/article/item/how_narcissistic_leaders_make_organizations_less_ethical

Collins, D. (2019, August 26). The Overt Narcissist – A Personality Disorder (adapted from my Linkedin article The Covert Narcissist: A Personality Disorder). www.linkedin.com. https://www.linkedin.com/pulse/overt-narcissist-personality-disorder-adapted-from-article-collins

cottonbro. (2021). Person Holding Red Heart Balloon. In Pexels. https://www.pexels.com/photo/man-hands-love-people-7670313/

Greenberg, E. (2019, February 11). How Do You Develop Whole Object Relations as an Adult? Psychology Today. https://www.psychologytoday.com/us/blog/understanding-narcissism/201902/how-do-you-develop-whole-object-relations-adult

Hammond, C. (2015, May 27). How Narcissists Use Money to Abuse. PsychCentral. https://psychcentral.com/pro/exhausted-woman/2015-05/how-narcissists-use-money-to-abuse#1

Huizen, J. (2020, July 14). What is gaslighting? MedicalNewsToday. https://www.medicalnewstoday.com/articles/gaslighting#gaslighting-examples

J, F. (2018). woman spreading her arms. In Unsplash. https://unsplash.com/photos/r2nJPbEYuSQ

Julie, H. (2017, January 18). The Overt Versus Covert Narcissist: Both Suck -. Narcissistfamilyfiles.com. https://narcissistfamilyfiles.com/2017/01/18/overt-versus-covert-narcissist-suck/.

Lamothe, C. (2019, December 16). Love Bombing: 10 Signs to Know. Healthline. https://www.healthline.com/health/love-bombing#takeaway

Launder, A. (n.d.). The Impact of Growing Up With A Narcissistic Parent. TheAwarenessCentre. https://theawarenesscentre.com/narcissistic-parent/.

Mayo Clinic. (n.d.). Narcissistic personality disorder. Mayo Clinic. https://www.mayoclinic.org/diseases-conditions/narcissistic-personality-disorder/symptoms-causes/syc-20366662

Mayo Clinic. (2017, November 18). Narcissistic personality disorder - Symptoms and causes. Mayo Clinic. https://www.mayoclinic.org/diseases-conditions/narcissistic-personality-disorder/symptoms-causes/syc-20366662

Muller, R. (2020). Gaslight. In Unsplash. https://unsplash.com/photos/odOKtrTX0Yc

Quirke, M. (n.d.). The Narcissistic Abuse Cycle: Idealization, Devaluation, Rejection. Michaelgquirke.com.

https://michaelgquirke.com/the-narcissistic-abuse-cycle- idealization-devaluation-rejection/.

Race, H. (2017). person standing near the stairs. In Unsplash. https://unsplash.com/photos/MYbhN8KaaEc

Sims, S. (2018). love shouldn't hurt. In Unsplash. https://unsplash.com/photos/3zgllN5P7Mc

Streep, P. (2016, May 24). The Communal Narcissist: Another Wolf Wearing a Sheep Outfit | Psychology Today. Www.psychologytoday.com. https://www.psychologytoday.com/us/blog/tech-support/201605/the-communal-narcissist-another-wolf-wearing-sheep-outfit

Your Mechanic. (n.d.). How to Find a GPS tracker in Your Car in 5 Steps. Your Mechanic.https://yourmechanic.com/article/how-to-find-a-tracker-hidden-in-your-car

Milton Keynes UK
Ingram Content Group UK Ltd.
UKHW020642230124
436534UK00017B/632